The Case of the Missing Planet

by
Jane Manners

Illustrations by **Elizabeth Wolf**

CELEBRATION PRESS
Pearson Learning Group

Contents

Detective at Work

Amy Lum wanted one thing. She wanted to be a detective. She wanted to be the greatest detective in the world.

Amy looked at everything. She detected everything. On her way to school one morning, she detected a cap lying on the sidewalk.

Amy noticed that the cap was red. Then she noticed a picture of a blue jay on the cap. "Hmmm. Red is Tim's favorite color," she said to herself. "His favorite team is called the Blue Jays."

Detective Lum had solved the mystery. The cap belonged to her friend Tim.

At school Amy gave Tim his cap. Then she looked at her teacher. Miss DeLuca looked back. She was watching her students. No one made a peep. Amy knew why. Miss DeLuca was trying to pick someone to help Mr. Cooper.

Mr. Cooper taught science in the middle school and ran the citywide science fair. Amy liked Mr. Cooper. He was nice, but the best thing about him was his dog, Frisky. Mr. Cooper took Frisky with him almost everywhere he went. He liked to joke that Frisky was his helper.

"Kate," Miss DeLuca said at last, "you may help Mr. Cooper carry our class science projects out to his van."

Kate jumped up and said, "Yes!"

"Rats," Amy muttered under her breath.

Mr. Cooper went back and stood by Evan's project. A blue and green ball hung from a string inside a large box with pictures of Earth and clay models of mountains and rivers around it.

Amy watched Mr. Cooper. When he leaned down to pick up Evan's project, she detected a dog biscuit in his shirt pocket. Then Frisky detected the biscuit. Snap! He grabbed it out of Mr. Cooper's pocket.

Mr. Cooper laughed. "When Frisky sees something he wants, he gets it," he said.

Amy thought about what she wanted. She wanted to be a detective. Her project was on the five senses and how a detective uses them to solve a mystery.

One day it would happen, she thought. She would solve a real mystery.

The Science Fair

That day after school Mrs. Lum took Amy to the science fair. Amy saw other kids from her class there.

Amy started down the first row. Some of these projects were pretty cool.

Amy saw Lizzie with her mother and her three-year-old brother, Mikey. Mikey twirled around, pretending to be an airplane. "Vroom, vroom," he said.

"Mikey," Lizzie's mother said. "Please stop that. I'm afraid you will knock somebody's project onto the floor."

Lizzie rolled her eyes at Amy, and Amy shrugged and smiled back. Then she started down another row. She saw a clock that ran on potato power and an aquarium full of different kinds of algae. She saw volcanoes, a collection of birds' nests, and a violin that played itself.

"There must be hundreds of projects in here," Amy muttered. She needed air.

Amy went outside. It was nice on the big lawn in front of the school. Mr. Cooper had tied Frisky to a big tree.

As Amy sat down under the tree, Frisky strained at his leash and barked at her. Amy tried to pet him, but he just stood there and kept barking.

Then Amy saw Jamal waving to her from the door. Something was going on. Amy ran back inside the gym.

Jamal, Mr. Cooper, and Evan stood by
Evan's project looking puzzled.

"What's the matter?" asked Amy.

Evan pointed to his project. There was
something different about it. "Planet Earth
is missing!" cried Evan.

3 Amy's First Case

"Do you want to know who took your planet Earth?" Jamal asked Evan.

Evan looked surprised. "You know who took it?" he whispered.

"No," Jamal said, "but I know Amy can find it. She's a great detective."

Evan looked at Amy.

Amy nodded eagerly as her heart began to race. Was this going to be her very first case? "I could find it," she told Evan. "I'll find clues and figure it out for you."

"Okay," said Evan, "but I can't pay you or anything."

"I'm not doing it for money!" Amy said. "I'm doing it for science!" She took out her notebook and started writing.

1. *Planet Earth was attached to Evan's project this morning.*

2. *Now it is missing!*

Think. Think. Think. Amy had to think. Evan's Earth was a little bigger than a tennis ball. It was blue and it had green parts for the land.

Amy decided to look at the string. She
took out her magnifying glass. "Hmmm,"
she murmured. It looked as if the string
had been torn, not cut.

"Where's Kate?" Amy asked. "Kate was Mr. Cooper's helper. She may remember something."

Kate stepped forward. "I remember watching the planet swing back and forth when we put it in the van," she told Amy.

"So," Amy announced, "the planet was still attached when it was in the van."

"I've got it!" Jamal shouted. "Let's look in the van."

Amy frowned. It was a good idea. She wished she'd said it first, though.

They all trooped outside to look in the van. Mr. Cooper took out his keys and opened the doors.

They looked and looked.

Planet Earth was still missing.

It was getting late. The science fair was closing for the day.

Amy found her mom inside. As they drove home, Amy looked out the window and thought.

The next day on the playground, Amy asked Kate some more questions. "Tell me exactly what you remember," she said.

"Well," Kate began, "like I told you, I remember seeing the planet when we put it in the van. Then we closed the doors, and Mr. Cooper started to drive away."

Amy detected a frown on Kate's face. "Yes?" she asked. "What else?"

"I waved to Mr. Cooper to come back," Kate said. "I had to run so he saw me."

"Why did you do that?" asked Amy.

"Mr. Cooper forgot his dog. He left Frisky tied to the post," Kate answered.

"So, Mr. Cooper is forgetful," Amy said, as she wrote in her notebook.

"Is that a clue?" asked Kate.

"Maybe. Maybe not," said Amy. She thanked Kate and closed her notebook.

That afternoon Mrs. Lum took Amy and
Jamal back to the science fair. Jamal
helped Amy search the gym. They looked
everywhere for the missing planet, but
they didn't find it.

"It was here," Mr. Cooper insisted. "I saw it when I brought Evan's project into the gym. I remember the planet swinging on the string, just like Kate said."

"Who else was here?" asked Amy.

"No one," said Mr. Cooper. "Just me and Frisky."

"What happened next?" Amy asked.

"It looked like rain," said Mr. Cooper.
"So I went down the hall to get my umbrella
from my classroom. Then I locked the
doors, and we went home."

Amy wrote everything in her notebook.

Amy looked around. The science fair
was busy again. Suddenly a voice rang
out so loudly that it made Jamal and
Amy jump.

Chapter 5 Digging Deeper

"Mikey, stop!" the voice rang out again. Mikey was pretending to be an airplane again, and this time his mother was mad. Mikey had knocked over part of someone's project.

"Come here this instant!" Mikey's mother yelled.

Lizzie looked embarrassed. Mikey didn't.

"Look at me!" said Mikey, zooming around. This time his mother grabbed him.

It was a good thing. Mikey was about to knock over a volcano.

Jamal pulled Amy aside. "I think I'm staring at a clue!" he told her. "Maybe Mikey knocked Evan's planet Earth off the string."

Amy looked at her watch. "Come with me, Jamal. I need to time something."

"Listen!" Jamal said. "Maybe he even pulled on the Earth and the string broke."

Jamal tried to keep up with Amy. "Little kids do stuff like that. He probably liked having the whole world in his hands!"

"Very funny," Amy said. She reached the end of the hall and walked back to the gym. Amy looked at her watch. She jotted down the time in her notebook.

Jamal saw Mikey, Lizzie, and their mother leaving. "Quick!" said Jamal. "Mikey's leaving. Let's talk to him!"

They went outside and saw Mikey trying
to pet Frisky. The dog was barking at him.

"Maybe Frisky saw Mikey do it! Dogs
are smart," said Jamal.

"It's not little Mikey," Amy told him.
"Let's find Evan. I know who did it."

Chapter 6 Amy Explains It All

"So, where is it?" asked Evan.

Amy looked at Evan. She looked at Jamal and Mr. Cooper. Then she opened her notebook and began to read out loud.

"Kate put Evan's project in the van," Amy informed them. She paused.

"Mr. Cooper drove the van here and brought Evan's project inside. Then he went down the hall to get his umbrella. But where was Frisky?" Amy asked.

Mr. Cooper scratched his head.

"Mr. Cooper had left Frisky behind before," said Amy. "What if he left Frisky behind again? What if Frisky saw the ball swinging on the string? Dogs like to play with balls. While Mr. Cooper went to get his jacket, Frisky had time to take the ball and run with it. I know. I timed it."

Amy took everyone outside. "Frisky buried the ball under this tree," she said.

"How do you know that?" asked Evan.

"When I tried to sit under this tree, Frisky barked at me. When Mikey tried to pet him here, Frisky barked at him. We were too close to Frisky's little treasure."

Amy pointed under the tree. The grass had been dug up. Dirt was showing. Amy dug in the spot. Soon she pulled the ball from the ground. Everyone gasped.

Mr. Cooper shook his head. "I'm so sorry, Evan," he said.

"I knew it was Frisky all along," said Jamal.

"It looks like it will clean up fine," said Mr. Cooper. "We can reattach it before the judges make their rounds."

"That's great," Evan said.

Amy closed her notebook and smiled. Her first case was solved.